The Writer's Notebook

Ideas for
Creative Writing
and Self-Expression

Grades 5–8

Written by Nancy Fox   Illustrated by Itoko Maeno

The Learning Works

Cover Design and Illustration:
  Itoko Maeno

Editing and Text Design:
  Clark Editorial & Design

Dedication

Thanks to Stephen Edele, the seminar students who read and fed this book, and The Pennington School for the research grant.

Copyright © 1998
The Learning Works, Inc.
Santa Barbara, California 93160

ISBN: 0-88160-312-0
LW 1013

Printed in the United States of America.

Contents

From One Teacher to Another

It all comes back, as everything always does, simply to personal pluck.
It's only a question, no matter when or where, of having enough.
—Henry James

"What shall I write about?" your student writers ask. The text and exercises in this book enable them to flip through the pages of their own days and ways and find—as writers need to do—their own A+ terrific answers to that question.

The Writer's Notebook adapts easily to your classroom needs and practices, whether you face an audience of 1 or 100 students. It can be used:

- as a complete writing program;
- as the writing component of a language or literature class;
- as an independent project for motivated students;
- as a guide for a self-directed writing course;
- as a series of exercises or projects for a teacher-guided writing experience;
- as the basis for both individualized and cooperative instruction, in the same class;
- as all of the above, and as you yourself devise.

Student writers should begin their writing course with the exercises in "Creating a Notebook" and end with the summary questions in "Conclusions." The two middle sections—"Creating Works in Progress" and "Creating the Portfolio"—lead to a goal. Each of these sections contains sequential text and exercises. However, the sections themselves may be used simultaneously. For example, one section might be classwork while another serves as homework or an independent project. They might be combined like this:

- Notebook + Works in Progress
- Notebook + Portfolio
- Works in Progress + Portfolio

The success of these exercises depends ultimately on the student writer's "pluck." But that quality, like language itself, is the human gift.

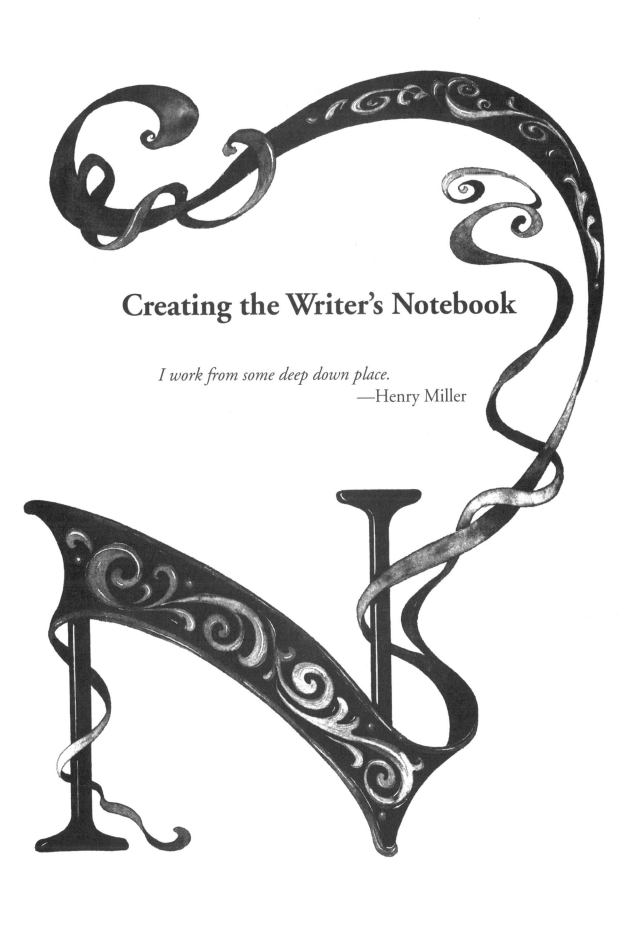

Creating the Writer's Notebook

I work from some deep down place.
—Henry Miller

To the Student

Like the physical spaces you call your own, the notebook is private. It contains the raw materials of essays and stories: the experiences, thoughts, sensations, insights, fantasies, and meditations of your daily life. Your notebook is the place where you confide the sentences which form in your mind at midnight as you try to sleep.

In the hut he built for himself at Walden, Henry David Thoreau placed his notebook paper under his pillow. He wrote his thoughts in the dark. Your notebook is the place to save those scribbled papers and scraps—like the matchbook covers and torn napkins where Francis Scott Fitzgerald scratched the phrases ("a voice full of money") that he later used in *The Great Gatsby*.

Feel free to grow, erase, cross out, reword, imagine a sentence a third or thirty-third time. Remember, if you can, the time and space you needed to learn to walk—and then to run, easily, with economy and grace.

"I'm a great believer in diaries, if only in the sense that barre exercises are good for ballet dancers," says the writer John Fowles. Your notebook will not be exquisitely neat. Life is not neat. If you have a specific project in mind, a deadline to meet, a topic that demands your attention and focus, these requirements will help you control those unruly thoughts and feelings.

Even in these more disciplined cases, if your notebook looks as if it has been trained in the Corps of Cadets at West Point, all spit and polish and so tightly written that you could bounce a penny on it, you are holding too much in reserve.

You should leave yourself room to move and flex your mind. Your notebook is that room. As you will soon discover, some issues you will encounter briefly. Maybe you will write a sentence or page and hit a real dead end.

Probably there are shoes in your closet that you loved for a week and now never wear. They pinched, or made your feet look like dolphins. Whatever. Other subjects will hold more promise. They will feel or need to be more useful. You learn how to live with them over a period of time. You break them in. You find how well they stand up to different weathers. You go with them. How many wearings make a pair of shoes unmistakably yours? You will need to walk a long way with some issues in writing. You will need to find and sustain a focus. The notebook is the place of departure: busy, noisy, destinations posted everywhere you look. You could reach anywhere from here. The big problem comes if you confuse this home base with one of those destinations.

"Obviously you haven't got a nice little road map," says the poet Ezra Pound. You will probably wish to arrive somewhere, finally. Although not every thought or experience you record can be shaped more formally, you may need to leave that private room and travel to specific points on the writing compass: a five-paragraph essay, a fully realized short story, a personal narrative, a letter, a poem, all points as different from one another as Key West, Florida; and Wood's Hole, Massachusetts; and Whittier, California.

You needed to start your journey from home, no doubt about it. Home is your identity, your personal moments, the place where you are the one and only. One cafe in Key West is wallpapered with its visitors' home addresses, ID cards, signatures. As a writer your notebook is home to you. You write there every day. You date your experience over a course of time living in this private property. But there are, for example, fifteen hundred miles to cover before a resident of Pennington, New Jersey, reaches that Key West cafe. And there are miles, more or less than that number, to travel between your notebook and your set destination.

"Of course, you need patience," says the writer Norman Mailer. Are we there yet?, you may find yourself asking, as we did as children, every five minutes, or paragraphs, or lines. Remember we asked that question because we were not in control of the miles or the vehicle. Signs to Boothbay Harbor, Maine; and Melfa, Delaware; and Tucson, Arizona looked green and rectangular and the same to us. But there is a difference in place we would certainly have recognized if we expected to eat lobster and swim, but found cornfields and granaries or cactus and desert instead. Therefore, like the child who nags and whines in the back seat and drives everyone in the car crazy, you need to move to the front and learn to read the map and recognize the signs. You accomplish this feat by leaving home—leaving that notebook—and taking your writing to a specific place on the writing map.

There is an essential difference between your notebook and the formal compositions of your writing. You may find yourself transferring whole passages from your notebook to drafting paper for an essay, short story, poem, or letter that you intend to present publicly. Or you may use only a phrase or spirit of a phrase. In the motion and play of your mind, the notebook is the necessary first act.

Truman Capote wrote six thousand pages of notes before he drew the first word of his first draft for the book *In Cold Blood,* the work he considered his masterpiece. That sequence of words—notes, draft, masterpiece—is one tried and true order of writing. You cannot tell the world what you know until you are aware that you know it. Your notebook speaks most eloquently to you. It is the Do Not Disturb place.

So, unless you already write with the daily discipline of a Dorothy Parker (and I for one do not), it's a good idea to keep that notebook. And keep it to yourself.

Note 1.

Whether it's spiral, red, or khaki, legal-sized, or a random collection of loose papers, your notebook should feel comfortable to you. It is your private writing environment, very much a writer's point of view.

✍ *Describe your notebook. Focus on the physical details, as if you were drawing it.*

Note 2.

The notebook will reflect your mind as it moves, plays, associates, connects, contradicts, observes, hits walls, lulls, leaps, lazes, casually serves up a gem.

✍ *Describe the physical place you will use for your writing this year.*

Note 3.

Your mind performs the random acts of thinking, and your notebook is a record of this perpetual motion. "It's our constant battle with nature, trying to subdue chaos outside and inside ourselves," says the writer Joyce Carol Oates.

✍ *What do you hope to achieve in this notebook? What do you hope will happen?*

Note 4.

Your mind, like most personal places, can be a wilder territory than the Serengeti Plains. In the space of one moment, your mind will skip from a headache to a cat with yellow eyes to friends for dinner to a blue dish of steaming blue crab to old age to a dog pressing on your foot to a slight shiver, and on and on.

✍ *Writing quickly, try and track the sounds you hear at this moment.*

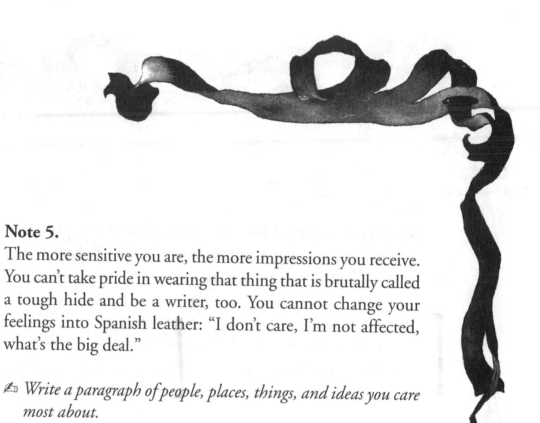

Note 5.

The more sensitive you are, the more impressions you receive. You can't take pride in wearing that thing that is brutally called a tough hide and be a writer, too. You cannot change your feelings into Spanish leather: "I don't care, I'm not affected, what's the big deal."

✍ *Write a paragraph of people, places, things, and ideas you care most about.*

Note 6.

You experience your moments, "the gusto and interest in every detail," the poet Marianne Moore reminds us. You feel the headache, hear the rumbling, feel the sudden chill. Any one of these impressions may reveal a hidden path.

✍ *Writing quickly, try to track the sensations you are aware of at this moment.*

Note 7.

Nothing is too small for the writer's observation. "In every situation hides some creative chance," wrote Robert Frost's friend Sidney Cox, an essayist.

✍ *Choose a detail in the room where you are sitting—something you don't think anyone else has noticed. Describe it. Why did* **you** *notice it?*

Note 8.

Here is a page from my notebook this summer:

No focus today. I listened to the hisses and shudders and groans of freight cars on the rusty tracks by the house. Wondered where they were going, why I was here, staring at white paneled walls and sun glinting on car fenders outside and a cat who stared back yellow-eyed as an owl . . .

✍ *Write a paragraph about your day. Start with a general description: for example, "No focus today . . ." Now prove what you've said.*

Note 9.

Just as an angel or magic spirit never appears to clean our rooms for us, no one will organize the wild things in our minds. We must impose order, that is, we organize the thoughts and sensations which are not orderly or even expected as we receive them in their natural states.

✍ *Take the paragraph about your day that you wrote in Note 8, select one event, and write one page about it. Try to keep your personal feelings out of your story.*

Note 10.

A cat who stared back yellow-eyed as an owl suddenly jumped on the end of a statement in my notebook about a restless day, a train. It came without warning or plan. I did not know how well I had focused on that cat until the words had sprung from the piece of felt at the tip of my pen.

✍ *Pick one detail from the description of the event in your day in Note 9, and write a page about it.*

Note 11.

Once upon a time every literate person wrote diaries and letters. In these pages they defined for themselves who they were and communicated with one another.

✍ *Do you ever write when you are alone? If so, what do you write? If no, what do you usually do?*

Note 12.

Imagine a world without telephones. Yet people have always needed to speak to one another as urgently as we do now. For us, these people defined the language and culture we inherited.

✍ *Imagine that you were without a telephone yesterday. How would your day have been changed?*

Note 13.

When people began writing novels, they often presented their stories as a series of letters and personal narratives, like diary entries.

✍ *Instead of calling a friend today, write her or him a letter.*

Note 14.

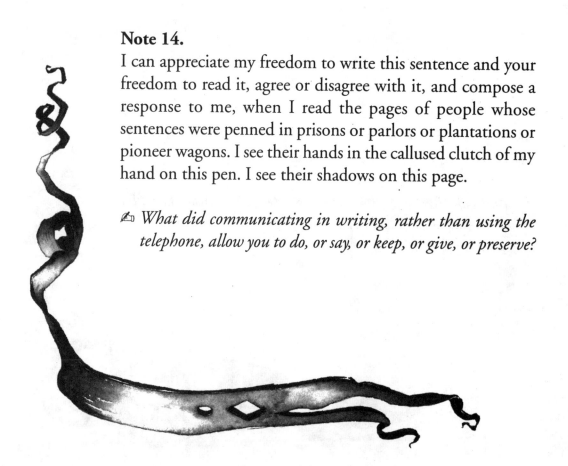

I can appreciate my freedom to write this sentence and your freedom to read it, agree or disagree with it, and compose a response to me, when I read the pages of people whose sentences were penned in prisons or parlors or plantations or pioneer wagons. I see their hands in the callused clutch of my hand on this pen. I see their shadows on this page.

✍ *What did communicating in writing, rather than using the telephone, allow you to do, or say, or keep, or give, or preserve?*

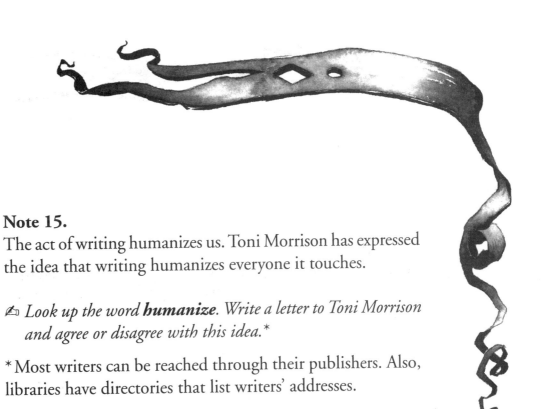

Note 15.

The act of writing humanizes us. Toni Morrison has expressed the idea that writing humanizes everyone it touches.

✍ *Look up the word **humanize**. Write a letter to Toni Morrison and agree or disagree with this idea.** *

*Most writers can be reached through their publishers. Also, libraries have directories that list writers' addresses.

Note 16.

In our time and society most people have an opportunity to be educated. Doesn't it seem ironic that most of us also allow machines—our cameras and radios—to speak for us, about us, to us?

✍ *Find a picture of yourself and lay it on the left page of your notebook. On the facing page, write whatever was happening in your life at that time that the picture does not reveal.*

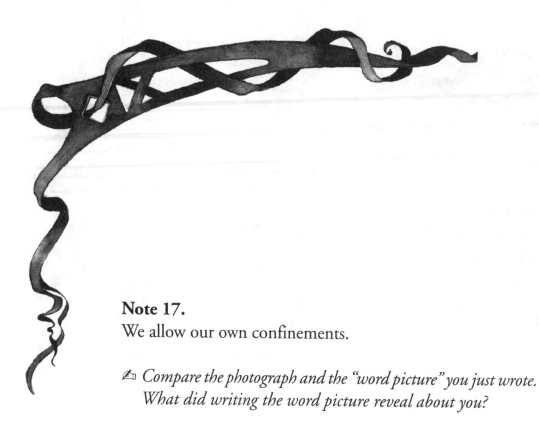

Note 17.

We allow our own confinements.

✍ *Compare the photograph and the "word picture" you just wrote. What did writing the word picture reveal about you?*

Note 18.

Could it be that most of the time we don't know how to begin to say who we are?

✍ *Who (when you look in the mirror) are you?*

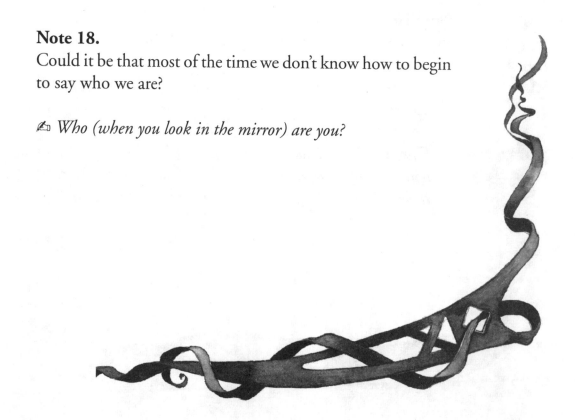

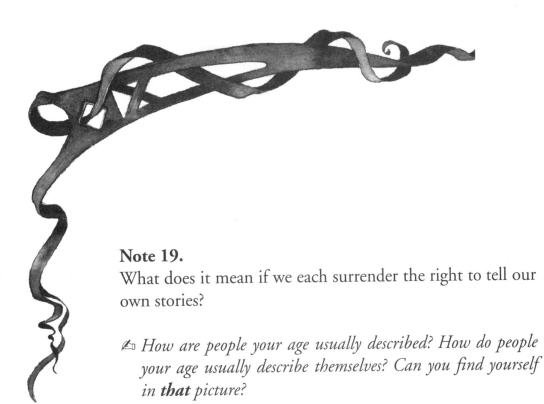

Note 19.

What does it mean if we each surrender the right to tell our own stories?

✍ *How are people your age usually described? How do people your age usually describe themselves? Can you find yourself in **that** picture?*

Note 20.

"We can't identify ourselves without stories," the writer Robert Stone says. "We're always telling ourselves stories about who we are. That's what history is, what the idea of a nation or an individual is. Who do we think we are and what do we think we're doing?"

✍ *Tell a true story about yourself.*

Note 21.

Your notebook is where your story begins.

✍ *Write one page: What have you been able to say in your notebook so far that you haven't said before?*

Note 22.

Your notebook reveals the conscious and unconscious elements of you—your plans and problems, themes and moods, styles and situations. It arises from that *deep down place* which is your point of observation.

✍ *Write about that deep down place.*

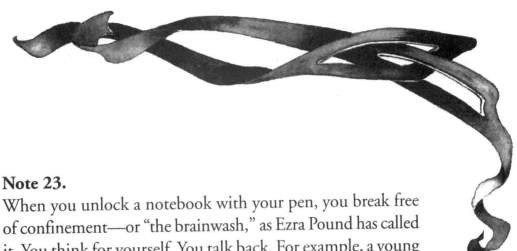

Note 23.

When you unlock a notebook with your pen, you break free of confinement—or "the brainwash," as Ezra Pound has called it. You think for yourself. You talk back. For example, a young woman in Alabama decided one day that she did not want to sit in the back of the bus where people called "colored" were told to sit. So she sat in the front where people called "white" were allowed to sit. Where is the brainwash here? That these people were identified and separated by color—until that young woman said "no."

✍ *Describe an experience in which you spoke up for yourself.*

Note 24.

You may not choose "the road less traveled by" that Robert Frost writes about, and pave that avenue with books written by the one and only you.* Nonetheless, you have a valuable course of life to define and make coherent.

✍ *If you were to write a book about yourself, what would be in it?*

* Read the poem *The Road Not Taken* by Robert Frost.

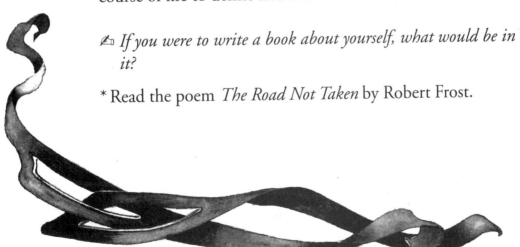

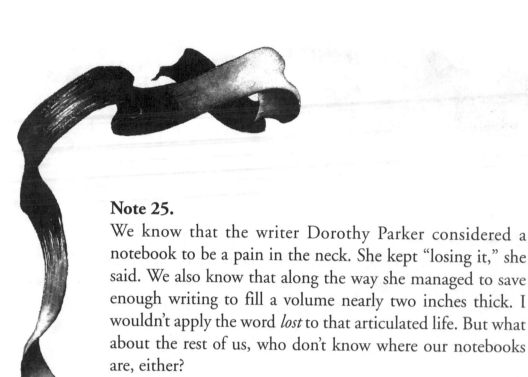

Note 25.

We know that the writer Dorothy Parker considered a notebook to be a pain in the neck. She kept "losing it," she said. We also know that along the way she managed to save enough writing to fill a volume nearly two inches thick. I wouldn't apply the word *lost* to that articulated life. But what about the rest of us, who don't know where our notebooks are, either?

✍ *Look back in the writing you've achieved so far. What experience or idea or feeling might have been lost if you hadn't written it down?*

Note 26.

"I can see that a loving care goes into my writing, which has nothing to do with writing as such but with the desire that what I have seen and known should not die, a sense of the preciousness of experience," says Anais Nin, in the 67th volume of her notebook.

✍ *What is the most important experience that you have recorded in your notebook and therefore preserved?*

Note 27.

As you sit there, feeling very cool and collected in your physical body, your hair washed and trimmed, your cotton sweater carefully selected, you are in fact working on countless levels.

✍ *Describe your physical appearance today: your hair, face, body, clothes.*

Note 28.

Some levels of you are as primitive and old as the human species itself.

✍ *Are you hungry? Are you thirsty? Describe your physical sensations right now.*

Note 29.

Some levels of you are hormonal and urgent, depending on your age and gender.

✍ *Are you restless? Is there perfume in the air? Do you have cramps? Describe yourself as a female or male, at this moment.*

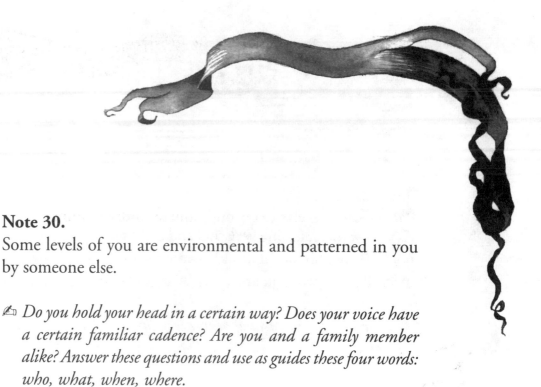

Note 30.

Some levels of you are environmental and patterned in you by someone else.

✍ *Do you hold your head in a certain way? Does your voice have a certain familiar cadence? Are you and a family member alike? Answer these questions and use as guides these four words: who, what, when, where.*

Note 31.

Some levels of you are psychological and buried by you.

✍ *What bothers you? What makes you feel safe?*

Note 32.

The intellectual levels speak of your education.

✍ *Write a page about your years in school.*

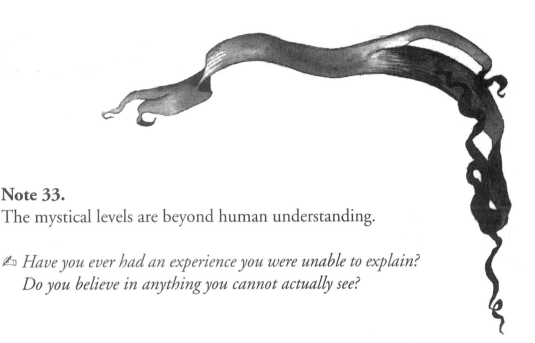

Note 33.

The mystical levels are beyond human understanding.

✍ *Have you ever had an experience you were unable to explain? Do you believe in anything you cannot actually see?*

Note 34.

Invisibly your skin is dying and regenerating, you are resolving a quarrel which hurt you, when suddenly you see in your mind the freckled face of a friend who moved to Atlanta, Georgia.

✍ *Describe a place where you would like to be right now, or a person you would like to be with.*

Note 35.

In the margins of your paper you sketch a chain of stars, absentmindedly.

✍ *Do you ever feel the need to sit and gather your thoughts? Try it now. Sit quietly, and on this page, gather a few thoughts.*

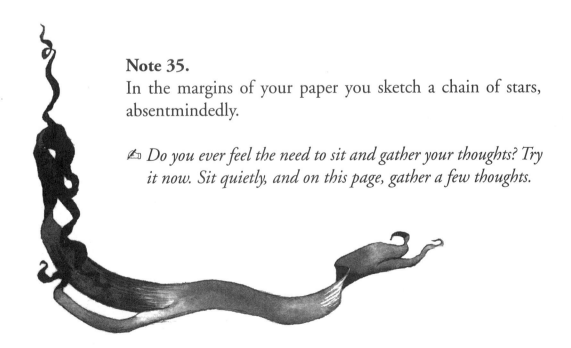

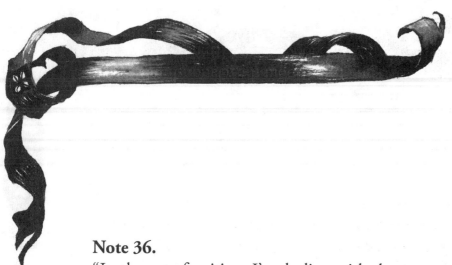

Note 36.

"In the act of writing, I'm dealing with the most primitive, elemental fears," says the novelist Francine du Plessix Gray.

Look up the words **primitive** and **elemental**. Describe an experience you've had when you've encountered those basic feelings in yourself.

Note 37.

Unlike an amoeba of a single cell, you are not a simple creature. Nor are you a little Mr. or Ms. Machine. You may feel that no one on planet Earth really knows you, and you may be correct.

✍ *Write about that feeling that all of us have sometimes: No one understands me.*

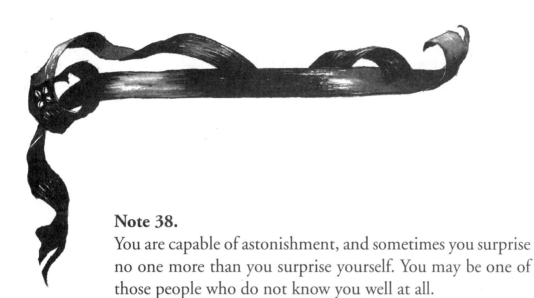

Note 38.

You are capable of astonishment, and sometimes you surprise no one more than you surprise yourself. You may be one of those people who do not know you well at all.

✍ *Describe an experience in which you completely surprised yourself.*

Note 39.

Your notebook is one of your answers to your doubts and your unknowns, whether the issue is "What am I?" or "What are you?" or "What do I think about the relationship between Huck and Jim?" or "What does Ernest Hemingway seem to think women are?" or "What are the faces of prejudice?" There are unlimited issues.

✍ *Write the date at the top of your clean page. Make a list of your own questions and doubts today.*

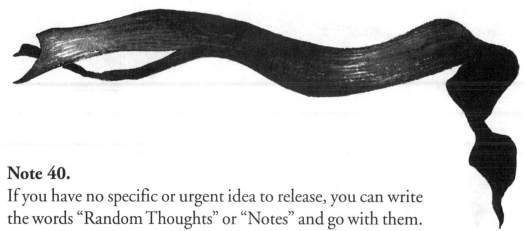

Note 40.

If you have no specific or urgent idea to release, you can write the words "Random Thoughts" or "Notes" and go with them. You might find one of these random thoughts is not so whimsical after all, and you have a page of "black on white," to use the phrase of story writer Guy de Maupassant.

✍ *Write random thoughts and start expressing them in phrases and sentences. Keep writing until you've filled one page.*

Note 41.

Other days you might awaken with an idea or feeling: write it down immediately so it doesn't dissolve in the crowds you will soon encounter. Then go away—to school, to work, to a friend's house—and let the notion work on you. The mind has a habit of doing this. The mind is wonderful. When you return to your notebook hours later, you might have a story to tell.

✍ *Try this: write down your first thought or feeling in the morning. Don't pick up your notebook all day. Then, at night, go back to your morning note and write one page about it.*

Note 42.

The poet Robert Frost tells us, "I use all sorts of things. Write on the sole of my shoe." One young writer jots notes on torn corners of old receipts, paperback books, tissues.

✍ *Try this for a day: take notes wherever you go.*

Note 43.

In the notebook you may find that all your notes can connect.

✍ *Take all your notes from Note 42 and put them together into a story. The story can be real or imaginary.*

Note 44.

The story of your day can achieve a coherence.

✍ *Take your notebook wherever you go today. Periodically write down what you see, hear, think, and feel, as you experience it. At the end of the day, write a paragraph that draws a conclusion about this particular day of your life.*

Note 45.

Sometimes the ideas or images are truly random and wild. Sometimes our most important thoughts develop in fragments over patient and slow time. Then you might consider the possibility that something large and still unseen by you is approaching, some change, some insight or realization, and all you have to do at this point is record its signals. If you are patient and watchful, the unknown will reveal itself.

✎ *Imagine that you are writing a book. What is its title, and what is your book about?*

Note 46.

"I write entirely to find out what I think, what I see and what it means," says the writer Joan Didion.

✎ *Write a page: "Here's what I see now, and here's what I think about it."*

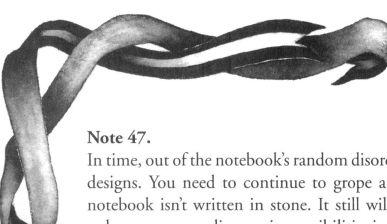

Note 47.

In time, out of the notebook's random disorder might emerge designs. You need to continue to grope a bit further. The notebook isn't written in stone. It still will evolve, and the only way you can discover its possibilities is to allow your pen to range freely.

✍ *Feel free to write a page.*

Note 48.

What you are doing is courting and charming your own mind and imagination. "A feeling of being in love" is the phrase many writers have used to describe the sublime thrill of finding a new idea at the points of their pens.

✍ *Write a page about being in love.*

Note 49.

Like all writers who have needed to breathe, eat, sleep, talk to friends—you have a brain. If you have used that brain, the writing in your notebook will be different from the work of any other person.

✍ *Look up the word* **unique**. *Write a page applying that word to yourself.*

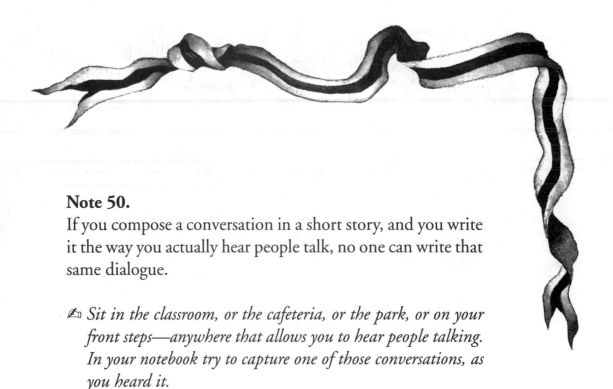

Note 50.

If you compose a conversation in a short story, and you write it the way you actually hear people talk, no one can write that same dialogue.

✍ *Sit in the classroom, or the cafeteria, or the park, or on your front steps—anywhere that allows you to hear people talking. In your notebook try to capture one of those conversations, as you heard it.*

Note 51.

If you are writing an essay on a character in a book—for example, Holden Caulfield or Makimba*—no one will feel about that person in quite the same way that you do.

✍ *Write a page about a character in a book. Describe that character as you see her or him.*

*Holden Caulfield is a character in *The Catcher in the Rye* by J. D. Salinger, available in most book stores and libraries. Makimba is a character in *Makimba's World* by Bobby Jackson, available through Multicultural Publications.

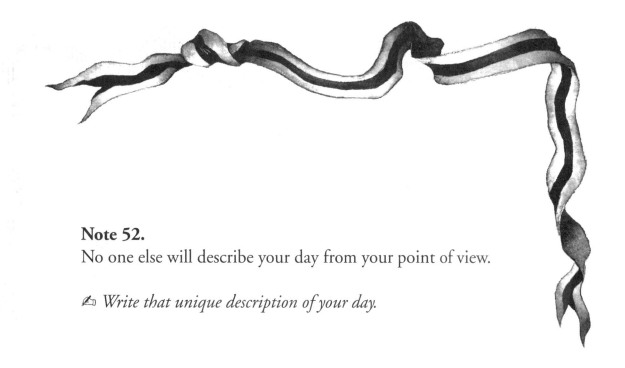

Note 52.

No one else will describe your day from your point of view.

✍ *Write that unique description of your day.*

Note 53.

If you are a born writer, you might find that your most important relationship involves the notebook on your table. Some days, you might find that you rarely speak to people. You listen or you dream. Your energy remains interior. When the pressure becomes too great, you use the notebook to release it. This, to you, is bliss. You know why writers fall in love with words, why Charles Dickens cried over his characters, and Franz Kafka laughed when he wrote his short stories, and Truman Capote read the dictionary.

✍ *What is your definition of a writer? Do you see yourself as a writer?*

Note 54.

But even if this intense involvement with writing is not your idea of a good time *at all*, your notebook will make your mind feel happier.

✍ *Write a page: "Here's what I accomplish in here, in my notebook, that I do not accomplish anywhere else."*

Note 55.

You might find yourself less and less capable of watching television, more and more apt to write better papers.

✍ *Describe yourself in the act of watching television.*

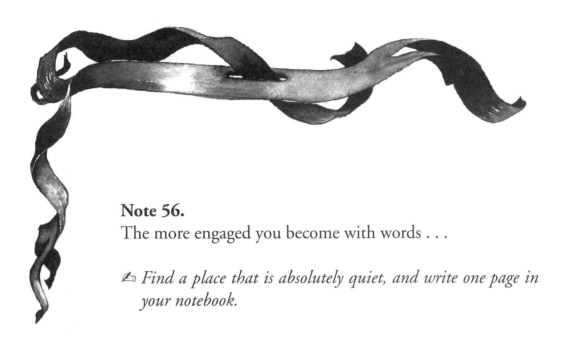

Note 56.

The more engaged you become with words . . .

✍ *Find a place that is absolutely quiet, and write one page in your notebook.*

Note 57.

. . . the less patience you'll have with noise . . .

✍ *Turn on your television and write a page.*

Note 58.

. . . the more ideas will come your way.

✍ *Compare the two pages—one written in a quiet place, the other written in the midst of noise. Did you feel any differences in the two experiences?*

Note 59.

"I have literally thousands of pages of notes here, raw, and I keep a diary as well," says the writer William Burroughs. "In a sense it's traveling in time."

✍ *Look back to the first pages of this notebook. Have you traveled in time?*

Note 60.

Keep your notebook. It will always be a good read.

✍ *Look through your notebook. Describe the ways it fulfills the hopes you expressed at the start. Describe the ways it surprises you. What have you learned?*

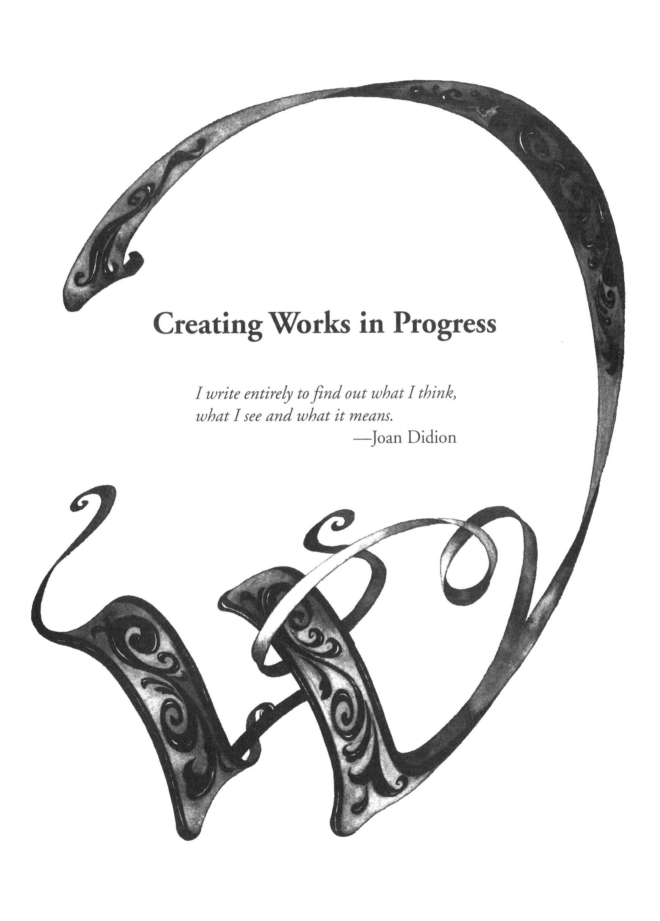

Creating Works in Progress

I write entirely to find out what I think,
what I see and what it means.
—Joan Didion

To the Student

I am the person who sits on a scratched and yellow library chair beside you. For the sake of convenience or convention you might look at my wire-frame glasses and tweed jacket and call me "writing teacher." But I remind you of two sentences that the writer William Styron said in an interview: "A writing course can give you only a start. It can't teach writing."

So I suggest to you that there is no such creature as a "writing teacher." The only real difference between us in this story is that I've spent more time in pondering, probing, and practicing the possibilities in writing. When I was a kid, I couldn't swim or shoot a ball through a hoop: what I could do was read and write (and ride a bike, which was green). Maybe I associate the color green with freedom. I always write in a green notebook now.

I have no method in mind for talking about writing with you: no structure, no formula, no philosophy that is original to me. I am one practitioner—pale, short, fond of writing poems on graph paper.

An untold number, since all their names and works are not known, have creaked these kinds of chairs in the millennia before us. I hope, for the sake of our children, yours and mine and theirs, that untold numbers will follow. I can't imagine a world without a person who sits in a private place and writes a line such as "You, pure and slender as a flame," or "I know why the caged bird sings," or "Now there is no place that does not see you. You must change your life." Although I have read as many written works as my eyes and time have allowed, I have found no ritual or magical formula to help me conjure an answer, *the* answer, to the question, riddle, story, which is writing. Every voice that has spoken to me from its characters on the page has defined itself differently.

Some of these works survive because they are historically powerful: "We hold these truths to be self-evident," "I went to the woods because I wished to live simply," "So long, so far away, is Africa," Other works are the supreme elegance of language, the pulse of experience, the laugh, the grimace, the cry, the lifted head: "I sang in my chains like the sea," "i thank you God for most this amazing day." There is at the same time the pressure of those voices, muffled, wordless, heard behind the door of history, which were not preserved. How do I choose? T. S. Eliot has said, "I've found that different people have different ways of working and things come to them in different ways."

And how do I have the right to choose? My judgments, as I sit next to you, are not more important than the discoveries I continue to make, as I read and write. Which writer do I choose to be *the* model?

Here is Henry David Thoreau, who wrote his essays alone in a cabin in Walden Woods and used a notebook, pen, maps, descriptions of minutes, soundings of a pond, thoughts about self and society. Over there is Henry James, who wrote novels in the palace of friends in Venice, surrounded by rococo paintings, who transferred this lush setting to heavily textured sentences on a writing desk the width of his forearm. Here is the poet Emily Dickinson, so shy, so seemingly starched in her white cotton, a woman who rarely encountered people in her life. There is story writer Ernest Hemingway, schooled as a reporter. Cicero, who spoke his essays. Alice Walker, who found a novel in letters. William Shakespeare, who composed drama in poetry. Who of these writers is the last word? Each, for reasons personal or political, has found a committed following.

What author would not be (perhaps unhealthily) pleased to hear, as someone said of William Shakespeare, that all other writing could disappear and only his remain extant, and still the depth of human passion would be represented? Yet, if any theme can be traced throughout the drama and poetry of this man, that theme is tolerance and more—a celebration of life's diversity and surprise. Do I, speaking to you of writing, do less than this? Do I narrow my sights, allow our time together to be an eclipse of your vision? "Follow your own patterns of feeling and thought. Accept your own life," the writer Katherine Anne Porter reminds us.

The writer's story is composed of the entire writing tradition. You will, as young writers have always done, make of this tradition what you choose, as you need or desire. But you will encounter the daily labor and sharpened pencils of Ernest Hemingway, the whimsical practice and yellow pads of Truman Capote, Toni Morrison's transcendence of death, the meditations of Annie Dillard, puzzles of Agatha Christie, poetics of Robert Frost—to name only six names from the bookshelves around us.

I can pick up a fragment of Sappho's lyrical poetry on parchment and form a picture of her in my mind: how she loved to write about people, I might say, and how true her imagery. The idea of wearing love as if it were a headdress! And Sappho died in a fall from a cliff 2,590 years before I was born in St. Francis Hospital, 7th floor, on a rainy Friday, as the poet Langston Hughes turned 50.

Within each piece of writing is, finally, a writer—idiosyncratic, editing as he goes, or not looking at the thing until she is finished and two weeks have passed, needing sunlight, needing a darkened room except for a single lamp, needing a library of busy people, a desk, a table, a lap, a listener, utter privacy, and an infinite number of combinations of these requirements.

"Writing has got to be an act of discovery," says Edward Albee. To suggest to you that the methods of one of these writers work any better than any other is false. The practice of writing is not the practice of method. It is the discovery of possibilities. In these pages you will encounter *writerly* voices. The word *writerly* in the world of books means that you enter the text you read and write it, too—feel anger or enthusiasm, open your workbook. That's the real introduction to the writer's story—you, your pen in your hand, giving that page a piece of your mind.

Work 1.

The writing you do—more than any other single act or possession—reflects you.

✏ *Let's call your notebook a "workbook" now. Fill the first page of this clean workbook with writing, and focus that writing on one topic only: your favorite blue painted shirt, your favorite person's left hand with the gold fingernails—something only you know about right now.*

Work 2.

Your writing is a mirror whose cold eye penetrates the simpler surfaces of you.

✏ *With your workbook, sit in front of a mirror. Describe the face you see, as if you were painting it.*

Work 3.

Your writing reveals the thoughts you think, the feelings you feel, and demonstrates with little doubt how well and how deeply you experience the life you were given.

✏ *What are you thinking, or how do you feel, right now?*

Work 4.

Your writing, held in a reader's hand and studied by that reader's eyes, will stand in place of your physical self.

✍ *Read a short essay, a newspaper article, a poem, or a story by a writer you don't know. Describe, in your workbook, the writer as you imagine her or him to be.*

Work 5.

"This is my letter to the world that never wrote to me . . . ," explains the writer Emily Dickinson in one of her poems.

✍ *Write a one-page letter entitled "My Letter to the World." If you wish, write it as a song.*

Work 6.

✍ *Describe clearly, in at least ten sentences, a familiar place where something important happened to you. Do not describe the experience—only the place.*

Work 7.

✍ *Narrate, on a new page and in at least ten sentences, the experience. What happened in that very familiar place? Focus on the **action**, rather than your **reaction**.*

Work 8.

Your writing is the document you leave: the letter you write to tell the world you were here.

✍ *Explain, on a new page and also in at least ten sentences, the importance of this experience in that place. What did it **mean**? And if you don't know, say so, and write about that feeling, which is a valid one.*

Work 9.

Anne Frank was a young woman who wrote a private diary.

✍ *Has the experience you've just described happened to other people? Can you form a connection with others through this experience?*

Work 10.

Do you suppose Anne Frank knew that you and millions of people would read of her bean suppers, quarrels with her mother, first romantic experience, fears of death, dreams of a home, menstrual cramps, photos of film stars, loneliness?

✍ *Go back to Work 6 and reread it ("the place"). Now, in at least ten sentences, make a connection between the place and what happened there—in the same way that Anne Frank's place had an influence on her experiences there.*

Work 11.

Your writing has a power beyond your dark-haired, light-haired self who lives in a house or an apartment, the self who eats pizza and owns a cat, a dog, a pair of jeans bleached to the blue of a dove's egg.

✍ *In Works 6 through 10, you composed a complete story about yourself. To whom would you like to give that story, and why would you like this person to read it? What would you hope to achieve, or change, or teach?*

Work 12.

If your writing makes sense, then you make sense yourself.

✍ *Open your workbook; sit very still. At this moment, in this place, what do you hear? What do you see? Write a page of impressions, sights, sounds as you receive them, right now, right here.*

Work 13.

You make sense of the world around you and give sense to the people who share that world with you.

✍ *Look up the word **sense** in any dictionary and write the full definition on a card that you paperclip or use as a bookmark in your workbook. Describe, in one page of writing, how that word applies to the story you completed about your experience.*

Work 14.

✍ Now, in a page, apply the word **sense** and its definitions to the impressions, sights, and sounds you tracked in Work 12.

Work 15.

✍ Sit at a window or on a porch or bench outside where you can observe a street. Track, in a page, the activity you see happening around you. Don't focus on any one particular event. Just let your pen skip around the scene.

Work 16.

✍ Now sit with the street scene that you recorded in front of you. Recall the atmosphere of that scene. Was it noisy? Serene? Write about the energy of that street as completely as you can.

Work 17.

✍ *The street scene is still in front of you. Choose a person and compare her or him to a character in a book you've read. (In what ways is that child playing in a small puddle like Huck Finn who played in Big Muddy?)*

Work 18.

✍ *Take the person you've just described. Write, in song form if you like, your person's thoughts in this place and at this time.*

Work 19.

✍ *Go again to the street scene in front of you. In a page, describe the ways in which the actions in that place celebrate life.*

Work 20.

✍ *Imagine that a child walks down the middle of the street you have just described. What does he or she make of it all, and what will he or she take from it all?*

Work 21.

✍ *Write about a problem on the street you've described: a serious problem for which there seems to be no easy answer. Then solve the problem.*

Work 22.

✍ *Write a poem describing the culture of one of your ancestors. End the poem in first person, with you observing that street in America.*

Work 23.

✍ *Write, in one page, the story of a sudden event that changed your life. Describe the facts of the event only. Hold your feelings back.*

Work 24.

✍ *Write, in a page, the story of what you did to move beyond or overcome or resolve that event.*

Work 25.

✍ *Look at the front page of today's newspaper. List the events in your workbook.*

Work 26.

✍ *Think about an hour in your personal life last night. List the events.*

Work 27.

✍ *Fit the lists in Works 25 and 26 together.*

Work 28.

✍ *Make a poem out of your lists.*

Work 29.

"There seems to be a kind of order in the movements of the stars and the turning of the earth and the changing of the seasons, and even in the cycle of human life. But human life itself is almost pure chaos," says the writer Katherine Anne Porter.

✍ *Look at your poem. Is Katherine Anne Porter correct? Is human life almost pure chaos?*

Work 30.

I think we call this chaos the "facts of life" and focus our attention on the brand of ice tea we buy, our date at 3:30, our sandals, our t-shirts in extra large sizes and bright reds, yellows, whites—all the *particulars* we see and touch every day.

✍ *Rewrite your poem: take one event from the newspaper and one event from your life, fit them together, and focus the poem on these two* **particulars** *only.*

Work 31.

We try to keep things in order, stay centered, get ourselves together: we have many useful expressions for this sane and serious need.

✍ *Describe a scene that is vivid in your memory: a thunderstorm that you watched from a porch last summer, a crashing wave that splashed over you, a room you made your own—green and white, linen and calico, black and sleek—and how you did it. Focus on color and texture. Hold your feelings back until the last sentence.*

Work 32.

The world does not make sense to us, it contradicts itself, and so we balance this apparent craziness by keeping a calendar, hanging up our clothes (eventually), making a kite, making a friend.

✍ *Write a very short and true story about the first time you did something: hit a home run, realized your parents were human, read a Shakespeare play, slipped and fell in public, made a dress, took one look at the quiet person with the brown hair and fell in love.*

Work 33.

The same need for order is the reason writers write. "You make little forms, like blowing smoke rings," said the writer Robert Frost.

✍ *In one paragraph describe a childhood scene or event that you can picture vividly in your mind. Describe it through your senses. What did you see, hear, taste, smell, physically feel? Write about the sounds and colors, the heat or cold, the salt or sweetness—the **particulars**—of that day. Try not to express your feelings directly.*

Work 34.

Frost told us, "I took the road less traveled by, and that has made all the difference." His road was a career of writing and discussing writing in schools and on television.

✍ *Find and read a Robert Frost poem. Read it two or three times. Read it aloud. Describe in your workbook the person you imagine Frost to be and the message you hear when you read his work. Frost believed that poets send their readers messages, and that the poem is like a code.*

Work 35.

You may choose that writing path, or not; it may choose you.

✍ *Take the childhood scene you wrote in Work 33. Break it into small lines, with one image or fact on each line. What have you got, poet?*

Work 36.

But whichever path you choose, unless you play solitaire in a room with closed windows and no door, you will need to communicate with other people who need order in their lives as much as you do.

✍ *Describe the midnight sky through the eyes of a teenage boy whose mother has just died. Don't discuss the mother or the death.*

Work 37.

A young woman named Kendall Hailey, who wrote her first book at the age of sixteen, believed that the words a writer gives to others might keep them from going mad.

☞ *Write a paragraph about a person you like very much. In your writing avoid the "foggy" pronouns (what, this, that, thing, something, nothing, everything, and all their cousins). These words are called **indefinite pronouns**. (That's their problem: they are **indefinite**.)*

Work 38.

Your writing has an effect. You are powerless to change that fact. Writing is dynamic and has been since the first human hand carved a symbol.

☞ *Sit at the window and draw (in words) a clear picture of a tree or a building so that someone reading your words could see it.*

Work 39.

The question remains: What effect will *you* create?

✍ *Write a letter to the school newspaper about an issue that deeply concerns you. Avoid the indefinite pronouns listed in Work 37.*

Work 40.

No teacher, no trick, no magic formula or ritual or muse can answer that question for you.

✍ *Now try writing a paper for your English, science, or social studies class without using indefinite pronouns.*

Work 41.

Only you can decide if you wish to reach other people and help them see more clearly, or cause them to close their eyes and fall asleep, or worse, offer them no hope for tomorrow.

✍ *Take one event from your list of newspaper stories in Work 25. Describe the problem and, in the second paragraph, solve it. Do not use indefinite pronouns. Send it to the editor of your school newspaper.*

Work 42.

You will either reach people or not, whether the writing at hand is a letter, an English research paper, a diary, a history essay test, a short story, a five-paragraph paper, a poem.

✍ *Select one piece of writing from your workbook and give it to someone—your brother, your best friend, your mom, your algebra teacher—to read. Write about how it feels to offer your writing to another person.*

Work 43.

Writing is writing. You as the author select its worth: "The right of every man to have his ideas judged one at a time," says the poet Ezra Pound.

✍ *Look up the word **abstract** and write the definition on a page in your workbook. Now describe your reader's reaction to your writing (Work 42) without using a single abstract word (love, anger, beautiful, terrible, intense). What did your reader do and say?*

Work 44.

If you respect the pen in your pocket, the instrument that waits to be held in your writing hand, so will others.

✍ *What did you do to cause your reader's nod of understanding or frown of confusion? Are you satisfied ? If not, what do you need to do?*

Work 45.

If you use that pen indifferently, your mind meandering to your weekend plans, impressing someone in the room, avoiding work right now . . .

✍ *Pick up your pen and let your mind travel with it. Write until you've filled one page.*

Work 46.

. . . the million distractions and entertainments that tempt us all . . . the red sports car in the parking lot, the extremely wonderful way a certain person walks, a certain person's sweatshirt, your new haircut . . .

✍ *Choose one scene, sight, or sound from Work 45 and try to describe it for an entire page.*

Work 47.

. . . the pen will betray you.

✍ *Read your writing from Work 46. Remove every fact and picture that does not relate to your topic. Rewrite every sentence that contains an **indefinite pronoun** and an **abstract word**.*

Work 48.

On the other hand, like a wizard's wand, your pen can conjure any one of those million sights, sounds, textures, thoughts, and feelings if you choose to learn its riddles and talents.

In a paragraph, describe a childhood feeling: "The blinds were drawn, the door was closed, and I was one unhappy four-year-old put to bed for a nap . . ."

Work 49.

It can make your experiences real.

Fill a page of your workbook with writing, and focus that writing on one topic from your day today: a cat with cappuccino eyes, a picture in this morning's paper, a comment someone made to you about your weight, a line from a song that you've been singing all day—something only you know about right now. And you know the types of words to avoid: indefinites and abstracts.

Work 50.

Only your pen has the power to unlock your hidden possibilities here.

Go back to your street scene from Work 15. Now describe that street scene from the point of view of a fourteen-year-old girl who has run away from home.

Work 51.

When I look at the pages of the workbook in front of you, I see the open door of the writer's story.

✍ *Imagine a character, male or female. This male or female has discovered a new skill or talent. Do not tell us this directly. Now have your character walk through a doorway.*

Work 52.

And what, after all, is the writer's story—if not the world as you experience and imagine it? Says Katherine Anne Porter: "I practiced writing in every possible way that I could." The best work in progress is the one you create yourself.

✍ *Write anything you want.*

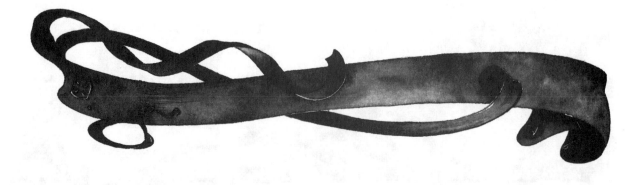

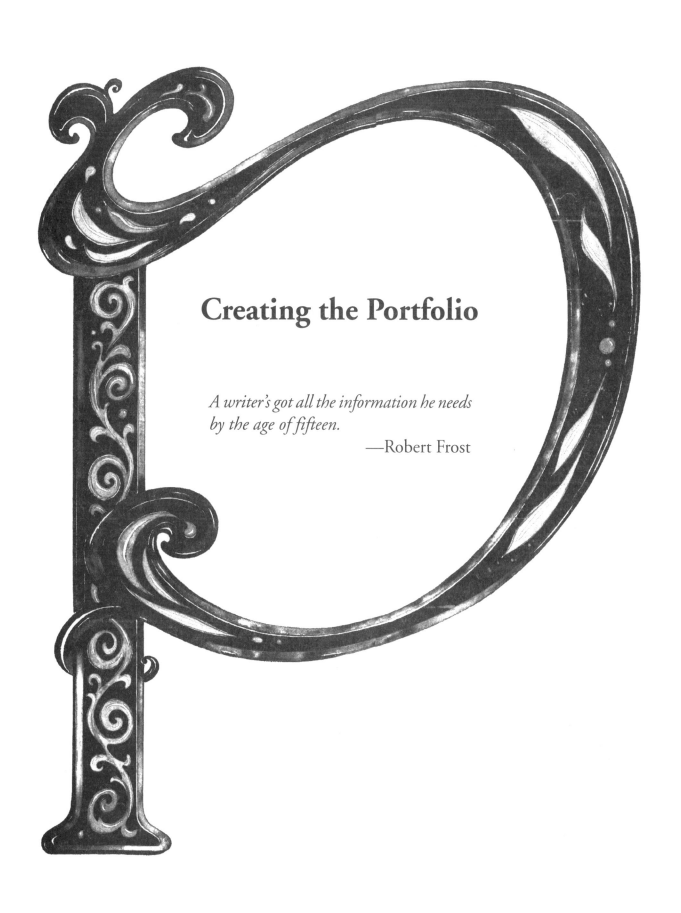

Creating the Portfolio

A writer's got all the information he needs by the age of fifteen.

—Robert Frost

To the Student

Ernest Hemingway kept a jar of freshly sharpened #2 pencils on a wooden counter where he stood to write. The implements you use are tools, and you should choose them as carefully as a captain selects his charts and an archeologist, her trowels. Your pen or pencil should feel comfortable in your hand. As a writer, your notebook and workbook are regular tasks, and composing drafts may be the "agony" that Truman Capote said they were for him.

Your pencil or pen is personal to you. It doesn't matter if the color is red, black, teal, or grey, when you are in the act of composing. No one but you will read this work. You may need to try every color in the school store until you decide that a black finepoint felt-tip will navigate your page most tellingly. Your drafts are always experiments, anyway. The final copy you offer for reading, however, is a different story.

Here your concern is not your own comfort or ease of creativity, but clarity of the lines and loops of your letters against the white background of the page. As printers have known for a few centuries, the easiest colors to read are black and dark blue. Your reader will not be entertained by red or lime green or purple words. They tire the eyes quickly.

The writer Gustav Flaubert, who penned Madame Bovary, advises us, "Be regular and ordinary in your life like a bourgeoisie so that you may be violent and original in your work." His wise words may be applied here. The excitement should be in the content of your writing, not in the flashy colors you use to write them. For your journeys here you should pack a pencil and black or blue pens, and some or all of the following equipment:

- a notebook for your thoughts, sketches, outlines, moments of experience
- drafting paper for your work in progress
- good paper ($8\frac{1}{2}$ x 11) for your final writing
- a calendar where you log your accomplished work
- a list of project ideas that will serve as a compass

This kit will allow you to navigate this course with as good a sense of direction as can be expected in the unpredictable territory of the manuscript. More technical equipment, such as a typewriter or word processor, will become necessary as you leave the zone of private pages and go public. Research papers and other major works are not handwritten.

In this computer age it's possible that your notebook is entirely on disk. It's a good idea here to make a backup on disk and print out a hard copy. If you have difficulty with spelling, use a dictionary or a computerized spell-checking program.

First and last, you are the writer. You are the one who will travel from the *writeable* to the *readable*. In the writer's backpack are guides to help you steer your course. They are your landmarks, signals, lighthouses, constellations. Their names are dictionary; manual of style; grammar book; thesaurus; manuscript format; and handbooks on writing short stories, poems, research papers, essays, and articles. Without reference to these guides (and most of them can be found on computer disks), no writing destination can be achieved.

Think of moving physically from one street to another, town to city, state to country. Without signs, how would you know where you were? How would you know the difference between a dead end and the address you needed? The same principles apply to your travels on paper. If you are to avoid becoming lost, you want to keep your wits about you and consult the signs.

The best guides are the works of people who have been there before you, who have seen the view from an essay, a short story, a research paper, a poem, a play, a novel, a newspaper article, who know the look and feel of those places. All together they are called a *library*.

Imagine a hairpin turn, a slippery curve, a road that ends in a cliff, a soft shoulder, a yield, a deer or train crossing, a shift into first gear for a steep climb, a narrow pass, a stall, a felled tree, a clean stretch of road.

Read the writers. They are your geography. Although the country you explore is uncharted, since you are yourself never completely discovered, the writers will teach you to recognize a big rock and a blackness of midnight sky. When you are lost in a fog or the dark, both seem the same.

Your journey here is writing. You do not know, and no one can say, the place you will reach at the end of your own writer's course. You can decide to travel in circles: *But I've always done it this way. . . . I have writer's block. . . . Give me a topic. . . . Tell me what to write about. . . . Correct this sentence for me.* Or you can decide to venture out. Explore. Experience. Attempt. Risk. Fail. Try another way. Find a way to get it in writing and get it right. To pass this course you need to write your way out of the circles and stalls and around the obstacles you will certainly encounter.

"I learn by going where I have to go," wrote the poet Theodore Roethke. Those words explain the writer's course, if you choose to take it, and the portfolio, if you choose to make it.

To Pick a Topic

I took notes on the people around me,
in my town, in my family, in my memory.
I took notes on my own state of mind, my grandiosity,
the low self-esteem.
I wrote down the funny stuff I overheard.
I learned to be like a ship's rat, veined ears trembling,
and I learned to scribble it all down.

—Anne Lamott

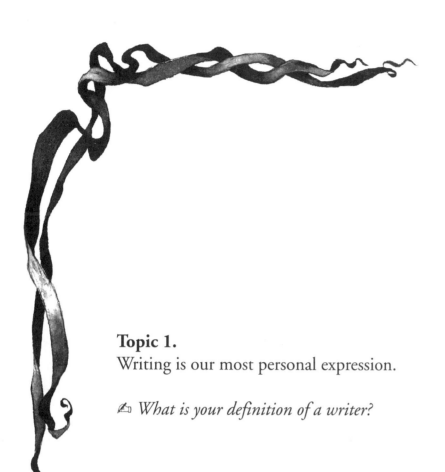

Topic 1.
Writing is our most personal expression.

✍ *What is your definition of a writer?*

Topic 2.
Writing is also a skill, a craft, a discipline, an art. There is an enormous difference between our diaries and an essay, poem, paper, or short story.

✍ *What is your hope or intention for this portfolio?*

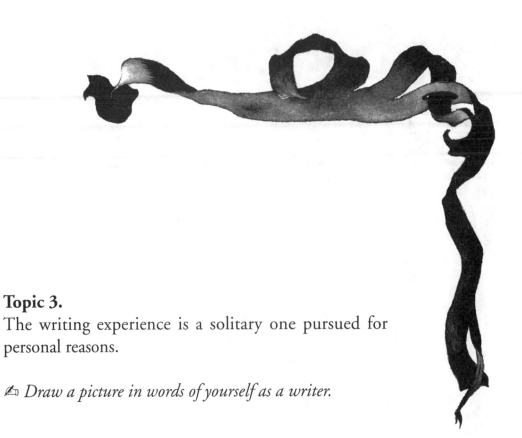

Topic 3.
The writing experience is a solitary one pursued for
personal reasons.

✍ *Draw a picture in words of yourself as a writer.*

Topic 4.
Often the piece of writing is important or necessary
enough to be offered to others. The *private act* is
transformed to *public art.*

✍ *What do you consider your major accomplishments in
writing, and why?*

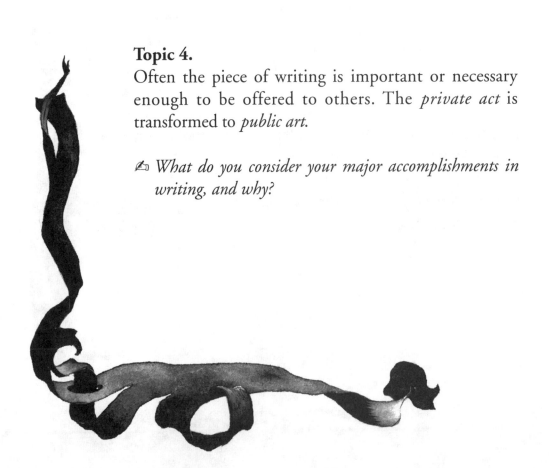

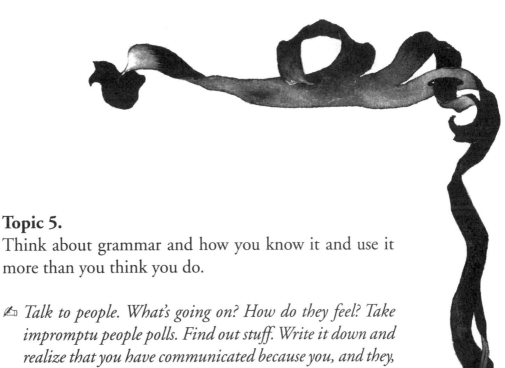

Topic 5.

Think about grammar and how you know it and use it more than you think you do.

✍ *Talk to people. What's going on? How do they feel? Take impromptu people polls. Find out stuff. Write it down and realize that you have communicated because you, and they, share a grammar. Your noun is their noun. Their verb is your verb. With those two words alone you can make not only a sentence, but a career: some writers refuse to use adjectives and adverbs. They rely on nouns and verbs.*

Topic 6.

Just as we have personal histories—once we were toddlers and now we are not—the words we hear have personal histories, too.

✍ *Look through dictionaries, papers, magazines, old yearbooks. What is new? What is interesting? What are your questions?*

Topic 7.

The word *grammar* became, in its adolescence, the word *grammarye*, which means *magic*. A skill in grammar was the same as a skill in magic, and the word *glamour* has grown directly from this notion.

✍ *Look around. Walk around. Take note and take **notes**.*

Topic 8.

Someone who knows how to use words creates a magical spell, a glamour, and transforms the ordinary stuff of life into a story that captivates and charms.

✍ *Sit somewhere. What do you see? Write about it.*

Topic 9.

Tennessee Williams magically calls us all from the crowded street into the room of his play *The Glass Menagerie* when his narrator says, "Yes, I have tricks in my pocket"—the same place where your pen waits, concealed, with the same weight as a key.

✍ *Get up in the morning. Don't talk to anybody about anything. Open your portfolio and start writing. ("Push that door. Open into the darkness. In the darkness I will find my unseen guide."—Sloan Wainwright) Stop . . . whenever.*

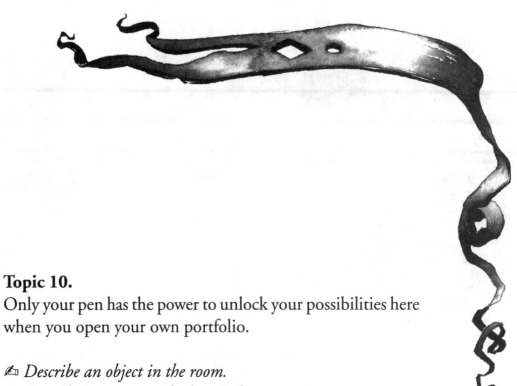

Topic 10.

Only your pen has the power to unlock your possibilities here when you open your own portfolio.

- ✍ *Describe an object in the room.*
- ✍ *Describe a scene outside the window.*
- ✍ *Describe an event.*
- ✍ *Describe a person.*
- ✍ *Summarize a short, factual reading.*
- ✍ *Duplicate a dramatic scene.*
- ✍ *Interpret a short reading.*
- ✍ *Be alone and make something up.*
- ✍ *Remember a moment.*
- ✍ *Imagine a future.*
- ✍ *Keep it all in a box, and when you need a topic, close your eyes and pick one.*

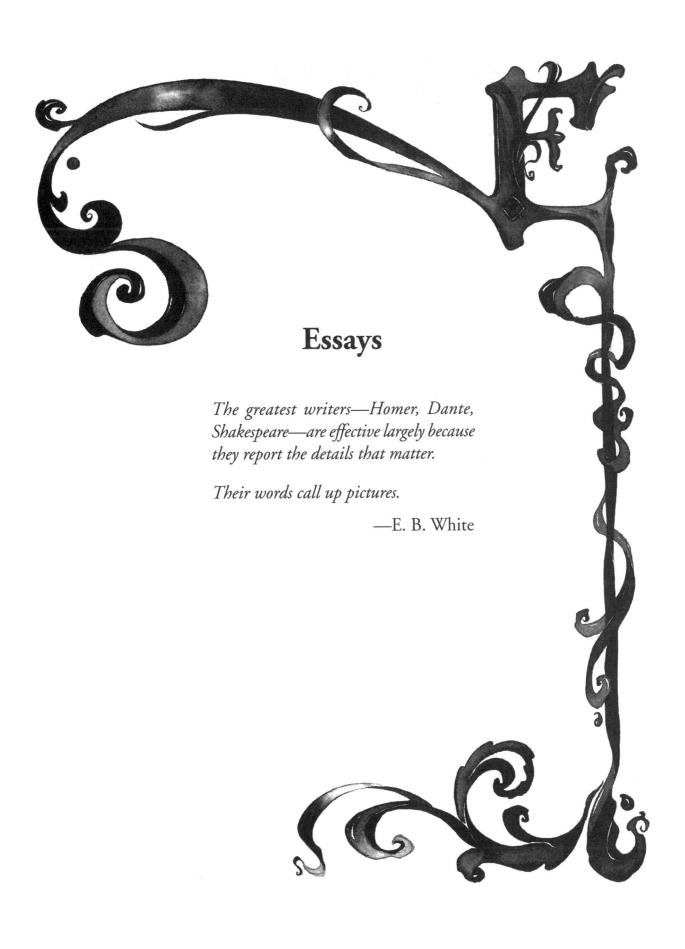

Essays

The greatest writers—Homer, Dante, Shakespeare—are effective largely because they report the details that matter.

Their words call up pictures.

—E. B. White

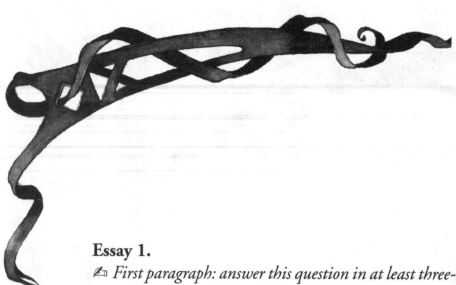

Essay 1.

☞ *First paragraph: answer this question in at least three-quarters of one page—clearly and excellently—as if you were writing the one and only book about this topic. What is **change**? Try, in your definition, to **compare** it to something else ("Change is like a stranger that sits in my living room one Sunday evening and refuses to leave") and s-t-r-e-t-c-h the paragraph.*

Essay 2.

☞ *Second paragraph: write at least three-quarters of one page. Where is **change** evident in the wide world? Try to **contrast** it with something **unchanging** (like one's addiction to Cajun french fries). Letting opposites play against each other is a great way to keep a paragraph—like a good conversation—spicy.*

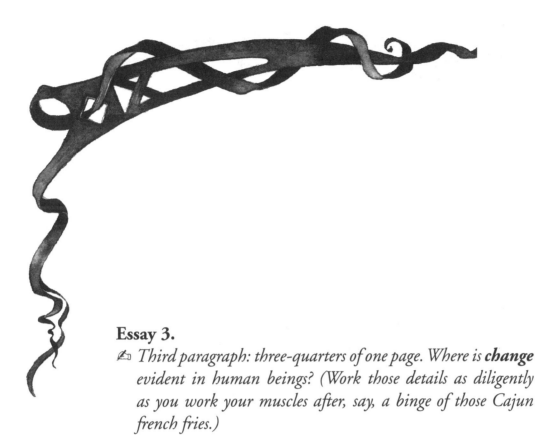

Essay 3.

✍ *Third paragraph: three-quarters of one page. Where is* **change** *evident in human beings? (Work those details as diligently as you work your muscles after, say, a binge of those Cajun french fries.)*

Essay 4.

✍ *Fourth paragraph: three-quarters of one page: what does* **change** *feel like in* **you**? *(Remember being twelve years old?)*

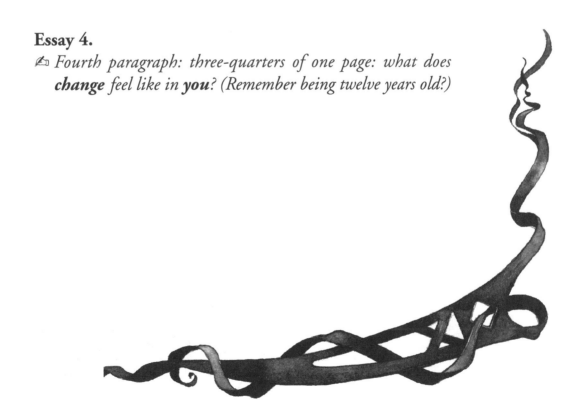

Essay 5.

✍ *Fifth paragraph: wrap it up. Why is **change** important, necessary, painful, decisive?*

You have now drafted a five-paragraph essay about change.

Essay 6.

✍ *Put your essay about **change** away. Don't read it or brood about it. Now spend a week pursuing a topic from your own list, one paragraph at a time. Feel free, though, to change the order of the paragraphs. Mix them and match them. Move them around. Play.*

Essay 7.

✍ *Remove your essay about* **change** *from its hiding place. Change it. Make sure it says what you want it to say as well as you can say it. Read it out loud, if necessary: does the grammar make sense? Is every word necessary? Does each paragraph present a picture? Does the writing have a point? Does it persuade? Does it charm?*

Essay 8.

✍ *Now put your other essay from your own box of topics through the same ordeal.*

Essay 9.

☞ *Type both of your essays. Make sure, either through the use of a spellchecker or a proofreader, that the spelling isn't a mine field of mistakes.*

Essay 10.

☞ *Put all of your drafts, revisions, and final copies in your portfolio.*

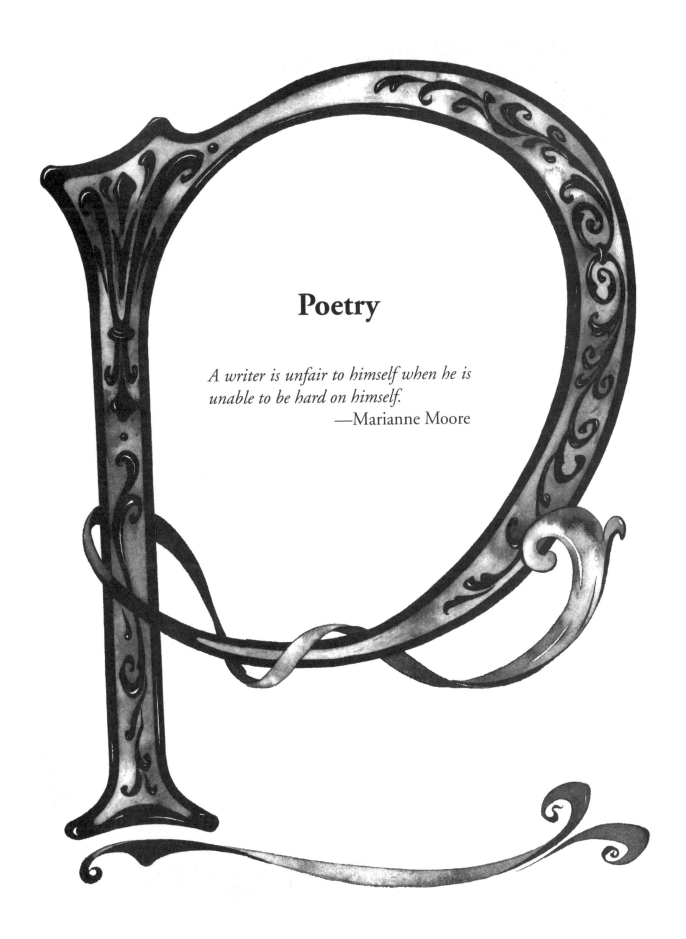

Poetry

A writer is unfair to himself when he is unable to be hard on himself.
—Marianne Moore

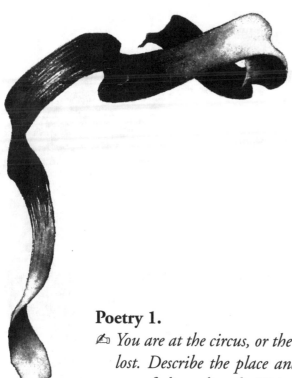

Poetry 1.

☞ *You are at the circus, or the mall, or a family dinner. You are lost. Describe the place and action without once expressing your feelings directly. Write ten lines with a word picture (or visual image) in each.*

Poetry 2.

☞ *Remove every "nothing" word (there, what, something, really). Remove as many "the's" as possible. Look up "adverbs" in your Big Grammar Book and remove them, like bulky sweaters in a warm gym, from your ten lean lines.*

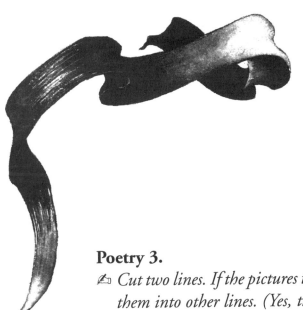

Poetry 3.

✍ *Cut two lines. If the pictures they contain are important, move them into other lines. (Yes, this is not easy.)*

Poetry 4.

✍ *Get this rhythm in your head: "Mary had a little lamb its fleece was." The rhythm is BOOM boom BOOM boom BOOM boom BOOM boom BOOM boom—exactly like the human heartbeat, a rhythm you've known since before you were born. There are five heavy beats in this line. They are: "Ma—had—lit—lamb—fleece." There are five dull beats in this line. They are: "ry—a—tle—its—was." Work this pattern, or meter, into each of your eight lines, if you can. Be utterly ruthless. Cut or move anything that breaks the pattern, known in the poetry circles you now inhabit as "iambic pentameter" (the heartbeat in fives).*

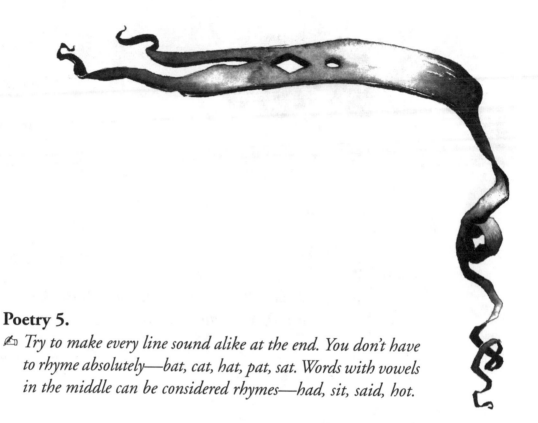

Poetry 5.

☞ *Try to make every line sound alike at the end. You don't have to rhyme absolutely—bat, cat, hat, pat, sat. Words with vowels in the middle can be considered rhymes—had, sit, said, hot.*

Poetry 6.

☞ *Get up and leave the circus or mall or family dinner. You are thinking about what happened to you. Describe what you see without once stating that you are experiencing a change of mind and explaining it. Write six lines with a word picture (or visual image) in each.*

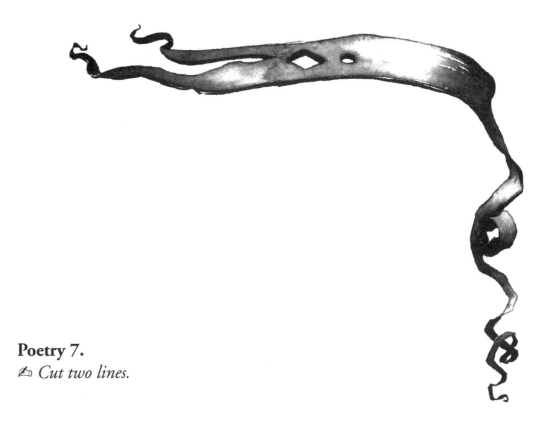

Poetry 7.

✍ *Cut two lines.*

Poetry 8.

✍ *Work the lines as you worked the preceding eight. Try to make each line contain five heavy beats. Try to make the lines sound alike at the end, without rhyming absolutely.*

Poetry 9.

✍ *Resolve the problem discussed in your poem in two final lines which absolutely rhyme.*

Poetry 10.

You have a sonnet.

✍ *Type and add your sonnet, with all its difficult drafts, to your portfolio. Now write a poem that's not a sonnet and add that to your portfolio, as well.*

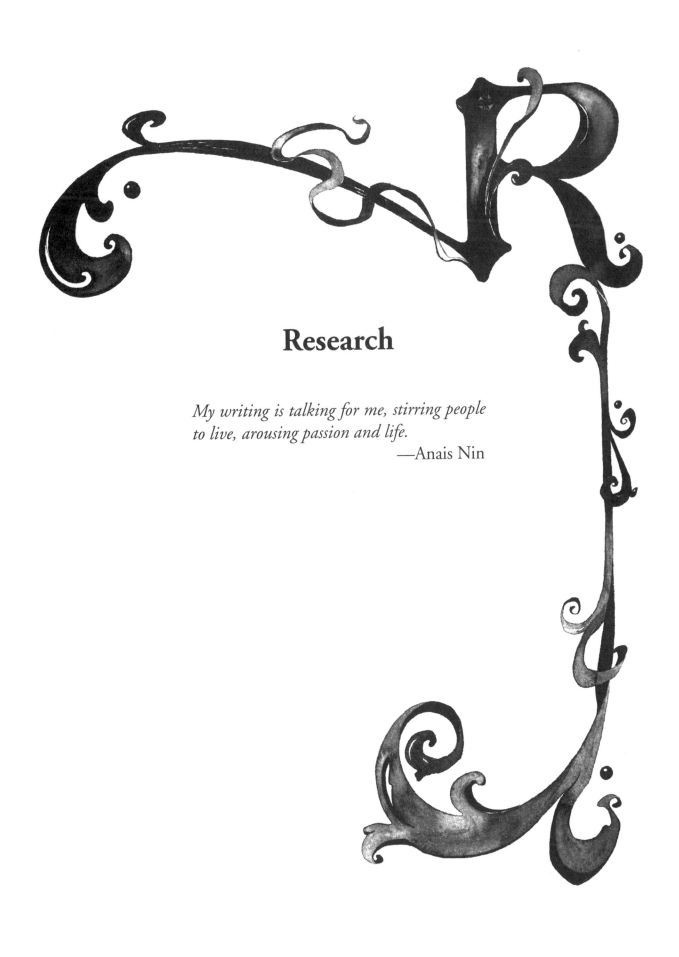

Research

My writing is talking for me, stirring people to live, arousing passion and life.
—Anais Nin

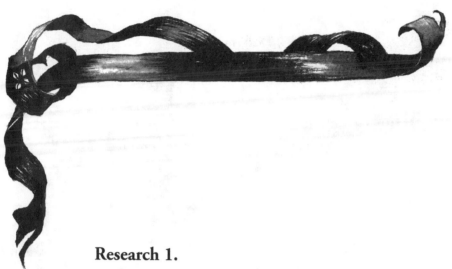

Research 1.

☞ *Suppose your topic is "bonsai," or "dance," or "rainforest." Find* **sources**—*books and articles about your topic—and list their names and publishing history on a page or on separate cards. Your Big Grammar Book or a guide to research papers or your English teacher will explain how to write these sources. Don't make up your own form: that's like making up your own definition of a home run: ("I do NOT have to touch all the bases!") Give each source a* **letter:** *easy as ABC.*

Research 2.

☞ *Read. Begin with* **large general sources** *(an encyclopedia, Who's Who, etc.). As you read, a* **small specific topic** *will catch your attention. ("Hm. Male ballet dancers. Rarity of. Why are they rare?")* **This question is the focus of your paper.**

Research 3.

✍ *Describe in a short paragraph the small specific topic you have found and the question you have asked.*

Research 4.

✍ *Your topic question is like an arrow. Now your research has a point, and you can start to direct your work to the sources, or parts of sources, that will answer your question. Note on pages or cards the most important facts and imaginings.* **Beside each note, write the letter of the book and the page number on which the note appears. Don't trust your memory.** *You're not just gathering notes; you're actually gathering* **your paper.**

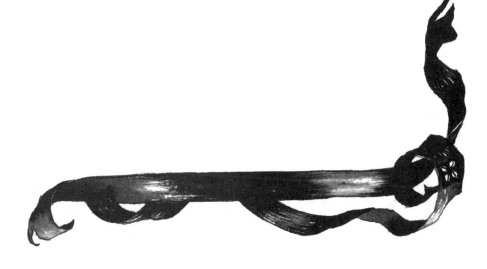

Research 5.

✍ *Place your cards or notes in order, from very large general information ("The rainforest is . . .") to specific information ("The acreage destroyed by 1998 . . ."). Now you can trace an* **outline** *for your paper. Write it down.*

Research 6.

✍ *Put your work away for now. Spend a few days writing shopping lists, sketches of people around you, songs, or sweet nothings.*

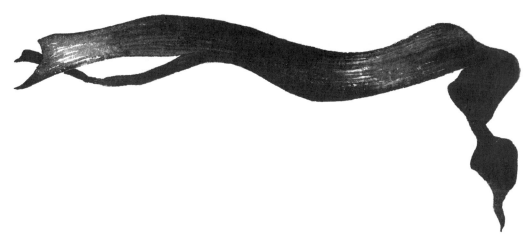

Research 7.

✍ *Begin to draft your paper. Follow the order of your notes. Remember to move from an introduction ("What is bonsai?") through proof ("Bonsai is often considered cruel because . . ."), to a conclusion ("Okay, here's why it's important for me to tell you this; here's why I care about it and why you should, too"). You may not know your conclusion until you actually get there. Use quotes from your sources liberally, and always give the name of the author who generously loaned you these words, the title of the source, and page number on which it appears: (Not doing that is called* **plagiarism**.)

Research 8.

✍ *Reread your report. Make sure your paper makes sense and proves a point. ("The rainforest is indeed vital to the survival of the planet.") Take out all your "I—My—We" statements and make them "It is clear," or "One sees," or "The perceptive viewer realizes, of course, that . . . "*

Research 9.

✍ *List your sources at the paper's end as you have learned to do; this is your list of "Works Cited."*

Research 10.

✍ *Type the final draft and put all of your working material in your portfolio. If you want to have a little fun with the paper, rewrite the whole thing in first person: "This is what I thought, then I opened books, or picked up the phone, called Belize, or Baryshnikov, or a bonsai farmer, and now . . . "*

Stories

Writing has laws of perspective, of light and shade, just as painting does, or music.

If you were born knowing them, fine. If not, learn them.

—Truman Capote

Story 1.

✍ *Be absolutely clear. There's nothing more deadly than a confused story. Make sure the reader always knows where the action is taking place and who is talking. Now, think of a story idea. Your story can be about anything: a girl meeting a guy, a relationship that's ending, a situation in a family. Write these facts now for yourself: who, what, when, where, why. Know more than you will tell.*

Story 2.

✍ *Tell your story from the point of view of one character. Describe this person to yourself, or better still, allow that character to describe herself or himself to you. ("So she asks me if I want to smoke some. I mean, like I really want to hurt myself, right? I've seen my friends get all messed up, their grades drop, they fight with their parents, they don't make sense when they talk, they're no fun anymore. And now I'm supposed to think that smoking this is some big special deal. If I have some, I'm a big man, right? She's digging her red nails in my arm. Come on, she says.")*

Story 3.

✍ *The most important thing is plot. Remember—you're telling a story. Don't put your readers to sleep. There has to be some interesting human problem which is resolved in some way. Write the last scene of your story.*

Story 4.

✍ *The story is told in actions and words—not explanations. Write the first scene of your story.*

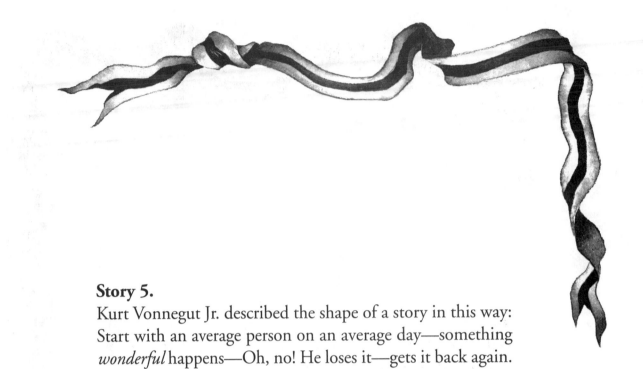

Story 5.

Kurt Vonnegut Jr. described the shape of a story in this way: Start with an average person on an average day—something *wonderful* happens—Oh, no! He loses it—gets it back again.

✍ *Look at your first and last scenes: describe for yourself the "something wonderful" and the "Oh, no!" problem that will lead from one to the other. You should now have a chart of four main scenes. Your finished story will be four to five pages in length.*

Story 6.

✍ *In your draft include a scene in which your characters express their feelings without speaking about them.*

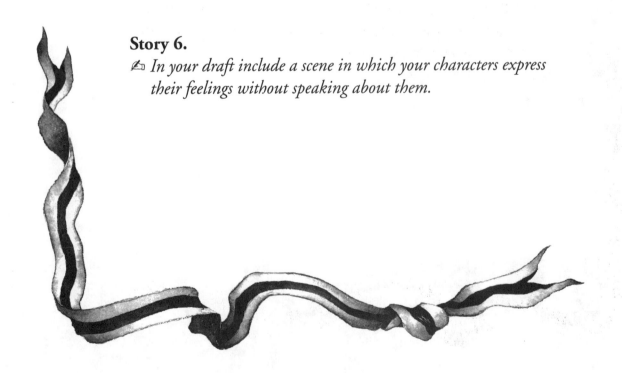

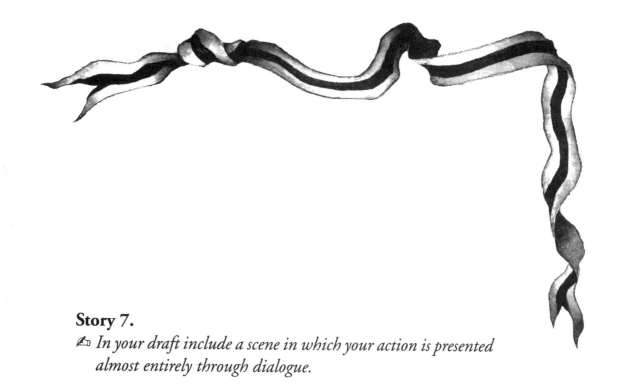

Story 7.

☞ *In your draft include a scene in which your action is presented almost entirely through dialogue.*

Story 8.

☞ *Try writing the story entirely in the past tense (which allows perspective and a thoughtful "now she knows better" tone). Try writing the story entirely in the present tense (which gives immediacy: how will this whole situation turn out for these people?) See which you like better, and make sure the entire story conforms to that time zone.*

Story 9.

✍ *Put your work away. Maybe write a letter to somebody you miss, or a poem that isn't a sonnet. Then take out your story and make sure it's a story: something significant has to happen, and your readers should be able to care about it.*

Story 10.

✍ *Correct your distracting grammar and spelling errors, type your story, and add this fictional "chapter" to your portfolio—notes, drafts, and all.*

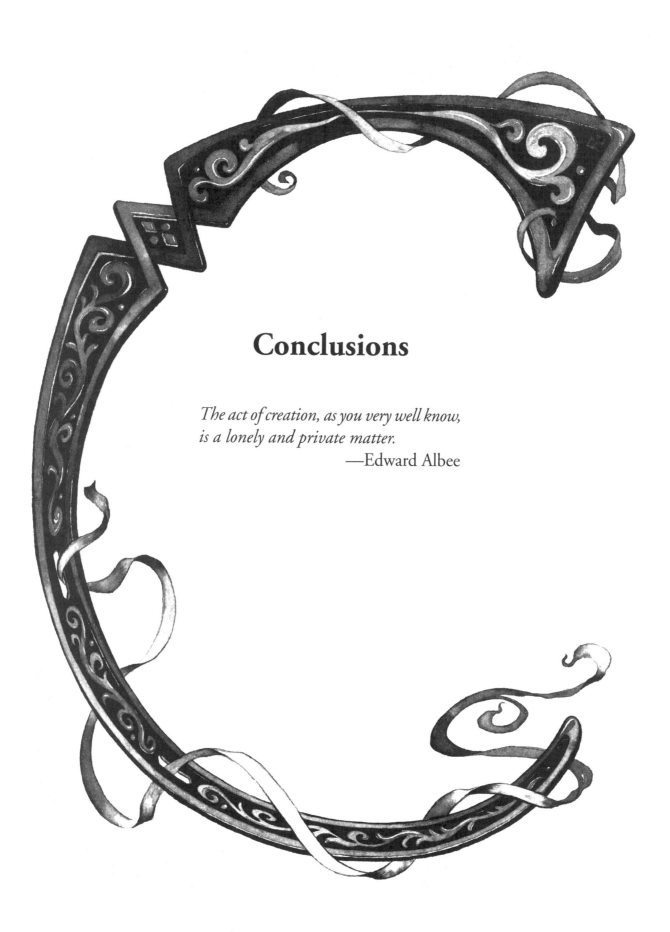

Conclusions

The act of creation, as you very well know,
is a lonely and private matter.
—Edward Albee

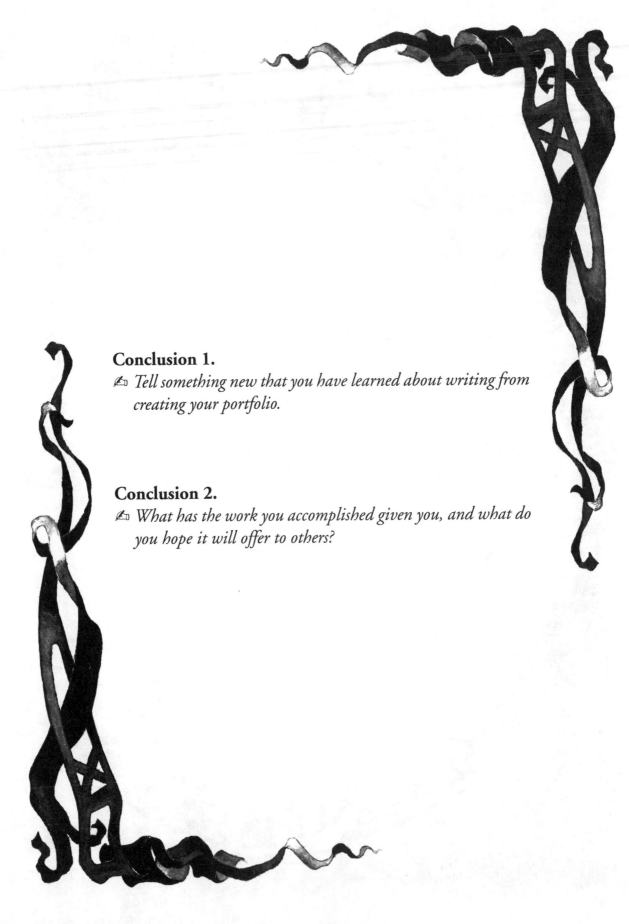

Conclusion 1.
✍ *Tell something new that you have learned about writing from creating your portfolio.*

Conclusion 2.
✍ *What has the work you accomplished given you, and what do you hope it will offer to others?*

Conclusion 3.

✍ *Which piece was easiest for you to achieve, and which was most difficult, and why?*

Conclusion 4.

✍ *Do you have new goals for your writing life?*

Conclusion 5.

✍ *As the last "chapter" in this portfolio, try something in writing that you haven't done before.*

About the Author

Nancy Fox is an editor, teacher, and writer. Her students have achieved portfolios, prizes, and publication. She is the author of the children's book, *Clarence When You Are Sleeping*, and her poetry and essays have appeared in *The Princeton Arts Review, Four Quarters,* and other journals.

She and her husband and son share a house with a changing cast of birds, books, cats, computers, dogs, family, fish, friends, and hamsters—all of whom were very present at one stage or another of the writing and editing of this book.